ICONIC NATIONAL PARKS

YOSEMITE NATIONAL PARK

BY EMMA KAISER

Core Library

An Imprint of Abdo Publishing
abdobooks.com

Cover image: Yosemite is the sixth-most visited national park in the United States.

abdobooks.com

Published by Abdo Publishing, a division of ABDO, PO Box 398166, Minneapolis, Minnesota 55439.

Printed in the United States of America, North Mankato, Minnesota.
052025
092025

Cover Photo: Paul D. Wade/iStockphoto
Interior Photos: Harshada Karnik/Shutterstock Images, 4–5, 45; Red Line Editorial, 7, 8; Aric Crabb/Bay Area News Group/MediaNews Group/The Mercury News/Getty Images, 10–11; CBW/Alamy, 12; Albert Bierstadt/Bridgeman Images, 14; Bettmann/Getty Images, 15; National Park Service, 17; Lee Rentz/Alamy, 18; Focus_on_Nature/E+/Getty Images, 20–21; Mint Images RF/Art Wolfe/Getty Images, 22; Bob Gibbons/Alamy, 24; Carrie Olson/Shutterstock Images, 25; Shutterstock Images, 27, 42 (top), 42 (middle), 43 (bottom); Jordan Siemens/Stone/Getty Images, 28–29; Andrew Soundarajan/Alamy, 31; M2 Photography/Alamy, 34–35; Tom Grundy/Alamy, 37; Quincy Russell/Mona Lisa Production/Science Source, 38; J. Bartlett Team Rubicon/Pacific Southwest Forest Service, 40; Alexander Demyanenko/Shutterstock Images, 42 (bottom); www.bazpics.com/Moment/Getty Images, 43 (top); Leonid Andronov/Shutterstock Images, 43 (middle)

Editor: Christa Kelly
Series Designer: Marley Richmond

Library of Congress Control Number: 2024948992

Publisher's Cataloging-in-Publication Data

Names: Kaiser, Emma, author.
Title: Yosemite National Park / by Emma Kaiser
Description: Minneapolis, Minnesota: Abdo Publishing, 2026 | Series: Iconic national parks | Includes online resources and index.
Identifiers: ISBN 9781098297213 (lib. bdg.) | ISBN 9798384919735 (ebook)
Subjects: LCSH: Yosemite National Park (Calif.)--Juvenile literature. | Mountain ranges--Juvenile literature. | Natural monuments--Juvenile literature. | Scenic landscapes--Juvenile literature. | National parks and reserves--Juvenile literature.
Classification: DDC 979.4--dc23

CONTENTS

CHAPTER ONE

REACHING THE VALLEY

Tallulah's family was driving through Yosemite National Park. A long road took them high into the mountains where thick forests of pine and juniper trees grew. The air got colder. From the window, Tallulah could see snow on the Sierra Nevada mountains. Then, the road started to take them back down. They were approaching Yosemite Valley.

The car entered the Wawona Tunnel. The long, dark tunnel cut through a mountain

With 214 miles (344 km) of roads, Yosemite National Park is a great place for scenic drives.

of granite. When they reached the end of the tunnel, the family parked and walked to the nearby Tunnel View overlook. Tallulah gasped at the scenery. The Yosemite Valley spread out before them. Mountains and forests reached up from the scenic valley. In the distance, a waterfall flowed down a granite wall. Tallulah was speechless. She couldn't wait to see more of Yosemite.

THE SIERRA NEVADA

The Sierra Nevada range runs along the eastern edge of California. It's more than 250 miles (400 km) long. The range begins in the Mojave Desert and extends into Oregon. The Sierra Nevada is home to giant sequoia trees, the largest trees in the world. Many consider the mountains to be among the most beautiful areas in the United States.

AN ICONIC NATIONAL PARK

Yosemite is one of the most famous national parks in the United States. It's located in east-central California, about 140 miles (230 km) from

YOSEMITE NATIONAL PARK

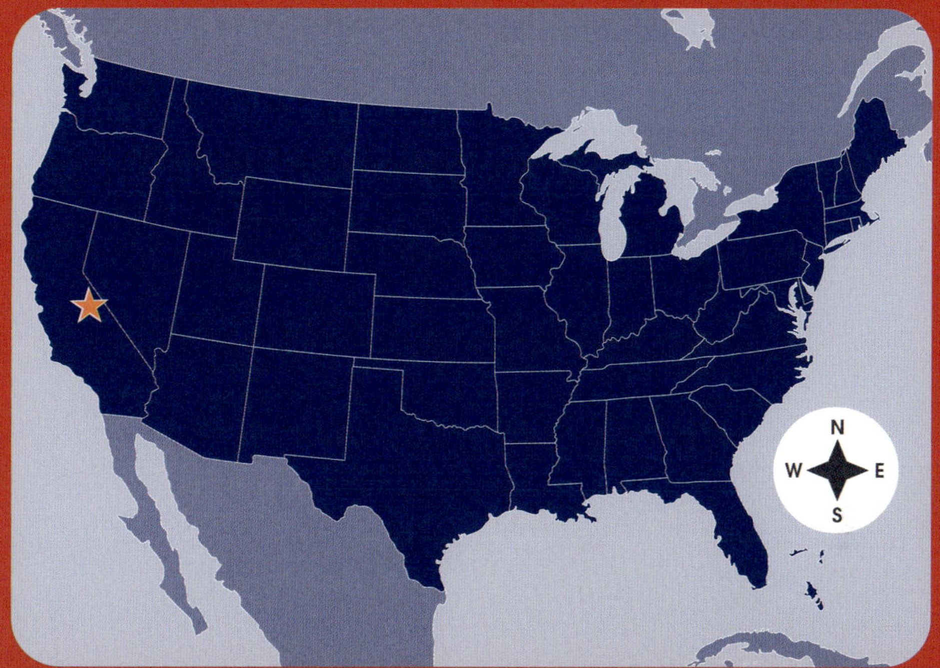

Yosemite National Park is located in east-central California. It's surrounded by forests and mountains. How might Yosemite's location affect the park's plants and animals?

San Francisco, California. The park is in the western Sierra Nevada.

Yosemite National Park spreads across 1,180 square miles (3,060 sq km) of land. It is surrounded by national forests. Ninety-five percent of Yosemite's land is designated as wilderness. This means it's protected by the US government and can't be developed.

INSIDE YOSEMITE

Yosemite National Park covers more than 750,000 acres (300,000 ha). It has a wide range of sites for visitors to explore. What are the advantages to visiting such a large park? What are the disadvantages?

1. Hetch Hetchy Valley
2. Tuolumne Meadows
3. Yosemite Falls
4. Half Dome
5. Crane Flat
6. El Capitan
7. Glacier Point
8. Wawona Tunnel
9. Yosemite Valley
10. Chilnualna Falls
11. Mariposa Grove

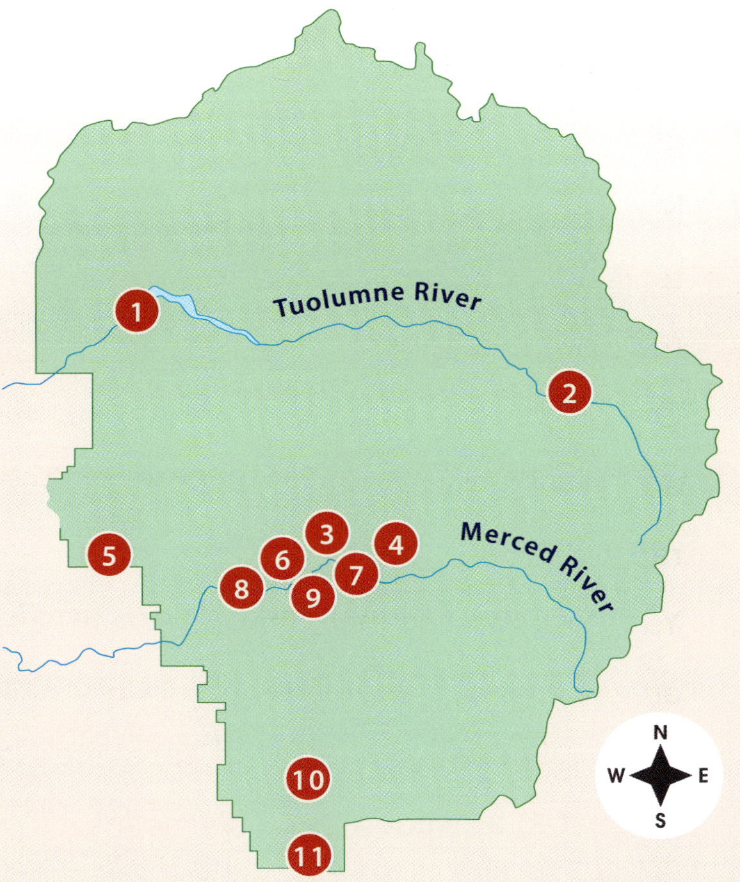

About four million people visit Yosemite National Park each year, making it one of the most visited national parks in the United States. Yosemite is known for its granite cliffs, stunning waterfalls, clear streams, and giant sequoia trees. Many tourists come to Yosemite to see the park's scenery. Others come to camp and hike. Today, park rangers work to protect Yosemite's landscapes and natural beauty for future generations.

PERSPECTIVES

AN ICONIC NATIONAL PARK

Yosemite National Park draws visitors from all over the world. Because of its natural beauty and recognizable landmarks, many consider Yosemite to be one of the most iconic US national parks. Scott Gediman is a public affairs officer at Yosemite National Park. He says, "Between the natural history, the [cultural] history, the wildlife, the beauty, and the size, there's so much to see and do in Yosemite. . . . It just encompasses so many of the ideals . . . that come to mind when people think of national parks."

CHAPTER TWO

HISTORY OF YOSEMITE NATIONAL PARK

The first people came to Yosemite at least 10,000 years ago. Among the region's first inhabitants were members of the Miwok nation. The Miwok are American Indians.

According to Miwok creation stories, the first Miwok people were created within Yosemite Valley. For thousands of years, the Miwok people lived in Yosemite. They hunted animals and gathered acorns. The Miwok built permanent homes and ceremonial buildings

The name Miwok translates to "People."

Mariposa County, the county that encompasses much of Yosemite National Park, was rich with gold.

in the area. Some of these structures were made of cedar bark.

THE CALIFORNIA GOLD RUSH

In 1848, gold was found in California. More than 300,000 people rushed to the region, hoping to get rich. Many of these people came to Yosemite. Some of the miners tried to claim the land for themselves. They killed thousands of Miwok people.

In 1851, an army called the Mariposa Battalion entered Yosemite Valley to remove the Miwok.

The battalion burned Miwok villages and tried to force the Miwok to leave the valley. The Miwok remained in the valley, but they had lost many of their people and most of their homelands.

The Miwok struggled to maintain their way of life. Some adopted European American ways. They started to wear European American clothing and build houses similar to those built by white settlers. Some traded with the white settlers or worked for white employers. However, the Miwok nation's numbers

PERSPECTIVES

MIWOK PETITION

In 1891, the Miwok nation sent a petition to the US government. The Miwok wanted money for the land and homes they lost in Yosemite. The Miwok people wrote, "The valley is cut up completely by dusty, sandy roads, leading from the hotels of whites in every direction. The head men of the whites also order their workmen to cut away the trees in every direction, and destroy the shade and beauty of the valley." The Miwok nation's petition was ignored.

Albert Bierstadt was a landscape artist. Some of his most famous paintings are of Yosemite.

continued to shrink. By 1910, about 90 percent of Miwok people were dead or missing.

As more settlers traveled through Yosemite, word spread about how beautiful the region was. Artists, painters, and photographers shared images of Yosemite Valley and the giant sequoia trees. Tourists made their way to Yosemite to see the beautiful area. Workers built hotels and inns to house the tourists.

The US government saw how important the Yosemite area was to the American people. In 1864, President Abraham Lincoln signed the Yosemite

John Muir, *right*, traveled to Yosemite with President Theodore Roosevelt, *left*, to advocate for the region's protection.

Grant Act. The bill placed Yosemite Valley and a nearby grove of sequoia trees under California's protection.

In 1868, a man named John Muir came to Yosemite. He fell in love with the region. He came to the area several times, sometimes working as a ranch hand or a shepherd. During his stay, he wrote about his time in Yosemite. Muir published his writings in newspapers.

He wrote about California's failure to protect Yosemite. Though the Yosemite Grant Act protected some of the region, much of the area was still in danger of being destroyed. Muir wrote about the destruction of forests and the damage caused by nearby livestock. Muir's writing helped convince the public that Yosemite needed more protection. In 1890, Muir's work paid off, and Yosemite was declared a national park.

VISITING YOSEMITE

Before cars were available, visitors came to Yosemite National Park in horse-drawn carriages. The first automobile was used in Yosemite in 1900. Automobiles quickly became popular. Roads were built inside the park, making the park more accessible. This helped the park become more popular.

MANAGING YOSEMITE NATIONAL PARK

For more than 20 years, the US Army managed Yosemite National Park. Soldiers battled forest fires and kept watch for trespassers. These jobs were transferred

Among the troops who protected Yosemite were the Buffalo Soldiers, members of Black regiments who worked tirelessly to preserve the park.

to civilian park rangers in 1914. Two years later, the National Park Service was created as an overarching agency to protect the nation's national parks.

As the park changed hands, the Indigenous people in Yosemite struggled to maintain their traditions. Many were forced to leave the area. The park service destroyed the last Miwok village in Yosemite in 1969.

Traditional Miwok bark houses can last for years.

In 2009, park rangers began working with local Miwok people to rebuild one of the Miwok villages in Yosemite. The rebuilt village had cedar bark houses, a ceremonial roundhouse, a sweathouse, granaries, and a chief's house. Today, visitors can tour the village and see how the park's original inhabitants once lived. The village structures are also used by Miwok people for ceremonies and gatherings. They help teach younger members of the Miwok nation about their culture and history.

STRAIGHT TO THE SOURCE

John Muir wrote many books about Yosemite. In one of his books, Muir said:

> *The famous Yosemite Valley . . . includes the headwaters of the Tuolumne and Merced Rivers, two of the most songful streams in the world; innumerable lakes and waterfalls and smooth silky lawns; the noblest forests, the loftiest granite domes, the deepest ice-sculptured [canyons], the brightest crystalline pavements, and snowy mountains soaring into the sky. . . . Nowhere will you see the majestic operations of nature more clearly revealed beside the frailest, most gentle and peaceful things.*

Source: John Muir. *Our National Parks*. Houghton Mifflin and Company, 1901, p. 77.

CONSIDER YOUR AUDIENCE

Adapt this passage for a different audience, such as your family or friends. Write a blog post conveying this same information to the new audience. How does your post differ from the original text and why?

CHAPTER THREE

PLANTS AND ANIMALS

Yosemite is home to a great diversity of wildlife. Hundreds of species of animals and more than 1,700 plant species can be found in Yosemite. The park has a large range of altitudes, supporting different ecosystems. Each ecosystem area is referred to as a vegetation zone. There are five different vegetation zones in the park. Each zone has different plants and animals.

The foothill-woodland zone is the lowest and driest zone. It receives no snow and is

Between 300 and 500 black bears live in Yosemite National Park.

Giant sequoias can grow more than 300 feet (90 m) tall. Their trunks can be more than 90 feet (30 m) around.

prone to droughts and fires. This zone supports native grasses and oak trees.

The next zone is the lower montane forest zone. This zone supports many kinds of trees, such as black oak, ponderosa pine, and giant sequoia trees. Giant sequoia trees are the largest trees in the world. They have massive trunks and can live for more than

3,000 years. There are three groves of giant sequoia trees in Yosemite's montane forest zones. These trees have shallow but far-reaching root systems. The roots absorb the melted snow that runs down from the mountains. This helps the trees survive hot summers.

Higher in the mountains is the upper montane forest zone. This zone is much wetter than the lower montane forest zone. It is home to pine and juniper trees as well as many kinds of wildflowers.

The next zone is the subalpine forest. This zone has long,

BLACK OAK TREES

Black oak trees were once abundant in Yosemite. For thousands of years, American Indians gathered the trees' acorns for food. They used controlled fires to help black oak trees spread their seeds. They also protected black oak saplings from animals. Over the years, scientists realized that the number of black oak trees within the park was declining. Today, scientists are using traditional American Indian methods to help preserve black oak populations.

Shrubby cinquefoil is one of the few plants that can survive in Yosemite's alpine zone.

cold winters and intense winds. Some species of pine and hemlock trees grow here but are often stunted due to harsh growing conditions.

The highest zone in the park is the alpine zone. This zone sits above the tree line. Only a few low-growing plants can survive in this area.

ANIMALS

Yosemite's diverse habitats provide homes for a wide range of animals. The park's range in elevation makes Yosemite a particularly great place for birds.

American dippers are normally found near rivers.

About 260 bird species have been spotted in Yosemite. Different birds are seen in the park during different seasons. During the winter, park visitors can spot the American dipper. This bird plunges under ice to hunt for insects and small fish. Other birds in Yosemite include owls, tanagers, and peregrine falcons.

Yosemite is home to about 90 species of mammals, including black bears, mountain lions, and bighorn sheep. The park is also home to many smaller creatures

PERSPECTIVES

BIGHORN SHEEP

Bighorn sheep used to live throughout Yosemite, but disease and overhunting destroyed their populations. The species eventually disappeared from the park. In the 1980s, a small group of bighorn sheep were brought to Yosemite in an attempt to restore their numbers. Now hundreds of bighorn sheep live in Yosemite's Cathedral Range. Sarah Stock, a Yosemite wildlife biologist, says, "Not only is the animal restored to its ancestral habitat, but we are restoring our personal connection with wilderness and what it means to be in a wild place."

such as fishers. Fishers are tree-dwelling carnivores with long tails. Habitat loss and overhunting have put them at risk of extinction. Scientists at Yosemite study the park's fishers. This helps them learn how to protect the species.

Wolverines are among the park's rarest animals. The animals were once thought to be extinct in California, but in 2008, a camera caught a glimpse of the elusive animal. Wolverines again went undetected in Yosemite until 2023 when a park ranger spotted one

Today, Yosemite is home to about 600 Sierra Nevada bighorn sheep.

of the animals in the park. This makes scientists hopeful that wolverines can still be found in the Sierra Nevada.

EXPLORE ONLINE

Chapter Three explores the plants and animals of Yosemite. The website below goes into more depth on this topic. What information does the website give about Yosemite's nature and wildlife? How is the information from the website the same as the information in Chapter Three? What new information did you learn?

NATURE AND SCIENCE

abdocorelibrary.com/yosemite-national-park

CHAPTER FOUR

RECREATION

Yosemite attracts millions of visitors each year. Some want to see the park's natural beauty. Others want to get active in the park. Whether a visitor wants to take a scenic drive or explore the park's trails, Yosemite offers something for everyone.

Sightseeing is one of the most popular activities in Yosemite National Park. Because Yosemite is such a big park, one of the best ways to see it is by car. Yosemite has several scenic drives that provide beautiful views of

Summer is the most popular time of year to visit Yosemite.

STARGAZING

Yosemite has very little light pollution, giving the area dark night skies. This makes Yosemite a great place for stargazing. People can see thousands of stars as well as the Milky Way galaxy with their naked eyes.

the area. One of the most popular drives is a 46-mile (74 km) stretch along the Tioga Road. This road leads high into the Sierra Nevada.

People can also explore the park on tours. Guides lead these tours and teach visitors about Yosemite's history. Bus tours and walking tours are available.

For those wanting to explore the park on their own, Yosemite has more than 750 miles (1,210 km) of hiking trails. Some of the most popular trails lead visitors to special sites such as Yosemite Falls or Half Dome. Others take visitors through scenic areas such as the Tuolumne Meadows.

Because Yosemite has so much to see, many visitors camp in the park overnight. The park has 13 campgrounds for visitors to choose from. All of the

Yosemite Falls is one of the country's tallest waterfalls. It is made up of three waterfalls.

sites allow tent camping. Ten allow recreational vehicles (RVs) and campers. Three accommodate people with horses. Visitors can also camp in Yosemite's backcountry. This requires a wilderness permit. There are also several cabins and hotels in the park.

GETTING ACTIVE

Yosemite offers lots of opportunities to get active outside. In the summers, swimming is allowed in most bodies of water within the park. Canoeing and rafting are popular in some lakes and rivers.

Bikers can enjoy the many bike trails in Yosemite Valley. Bikes are also allowed on most roads within the park. Visitors can bring their own bikes or rent them inside the park.

In the winter, hiking trails become covered in snow and are opened to cross-country skiers and snowshoers.

PERSPECTIVES

BEAUTIFUL INSPIRATION

Photographers and artists have been inspired by Yosemite for decades. Many come to the park to take pictures, sketch, and paint. Cleo Vilett is a landscape painter. She says, "[Yosemite] has endless possible subject matter. . . . No matter how many paintings have been done, or how many people have stood in awe in front of Half Dome or Valley View, the novelty never wears off. It takes my breath away every time!"

Badger Pass Ski Area in southern Yosemite offers downhill skiing and snowboarding. An ice rink is open to skaters in Yosemite Valley.

Rock climbing is another popular activity in Yosemite. Many consider the park to be one of the best climbing spots in the world. Some people climb with ropes and harnesses, while others prefer bouldering. Bouldering is climbing shorter routes without ropes. The most advanced climbers test themselves with difficult routes up El Capitan or Half Dome.

FURTHER EVIDENCE

Chapter Four discusses some of the activities that visitors enjoy in the park. What was one of the main points of this chapter? What key evidence supports this point? Read the article at the website below. Does the information on the website support this point? Or does it present new evidence?

THINGS TO DO

abdocorelibrary.com/yosemite-national-park

RANGER
RANGER

CHAPTER FIVE

CARING FOR THE PARK

One of the most important parts of caring for Yosemite National Park is making sure its various ecosystems stay healthy. Park rangers protect the park's meadows, wetlands, forests, lakes, and rivers. They also make sure that the relationships between the ecosystems' organisms stay in balance.

Humans play an important role in preserving the park's ecosystems. Often, human activities can damage natural landscapes.

More than 450 workers are employed at Yosemite year-round.

PERSPECTIVES

ACKERSON MEADOW

Ackerson Meadow was the site of one of Yosemite's most recent restoration projects. The area was previously logged for trees and used to graze cattle. Without native plants, the soil started to erode. In 2024, park workers grew native plants in the meadow to make the area a better habitat for pollinators. Tim Kuhn worked as a biologist for Yosemite. He said, "This restoration project is really helping the land become naturalized to what it was before. Restoring the habitat is really important to the park."

But humans are also capable of restoring and protecting natural spaces.

RESTORATION PROJECTS

Many ecological restoration projects have taken place in Yosemite. The goal of these projects is to help heal and protect ecosystems while still allowing visitors to enjoy the area. One of the park's biggest projects was the wetland restoration project in Yosemite Valley. This project focused on restoring wetlands near

Yosemite's wetlands provide homes for many species, including the endangered Sierra Nevada mountain yellow-legged frog.

Lower River Amphitheater. Human trails and other structures had caused damage to the area. The trail was preventing water flow and trampling vegetation. Invasive plants were hurting the ecosystem.

In order to restore the wetlands, a large section of trail was removed from the area. It was replaced with a raised boardwalk that allowed water to flow more freely. Pavement and other artificial materials were removed. Then, park workers replaced the invasive plants with native plants. By the end of the project, the wetlands

Despite growing into massive trees, giant sequoia seeds are tiny. About 230 seeds are packed into each cone.

were healthier and better able to support the animals that depended on the habitat. People were also able to visit the area without causing damage.

USING FIRE

Wildfires can devastate areas, but sometimes these fires are necessary for keeping ecosystems healthy.

Some fires are caused by people, but other wildfires happen naturally, such as when lightning strikes. Many species, such as giant sequoia trees, depend on fire. The heat causes the pinecones on sequoia branches to open, allowing them to spread their seeds. Fire also burns dead vegetation and helps clear the forest floor. This allows sequoia seeds to get the space and sunlight they need to grow.

Yosemite's first inhabitants understood that fire was necessary to keep the environment healthy. For hundreds of years, Indigenous people used fire as a tool to improve forest habitats.

MARIPOSA GROVE OF GIANT SEQUOIAS

The Mariposa Grove of Giant Sequoias contains about 500 giant sequoia trees and is a popular destination in Yosemite. However, the many visitors were harming the trees. Roads, parking lots, buildings, and trails can damage sequoias' root systems. The Mariposa Grove restoration project moved these structures farther away to protect the trees. This project was completed in 2018.

Controlled burns help native plants flourish.

When European Americans came to Yosemite, they thought fire was harmful and stopped all burnings.

Eventually, scientists realized that giant sequoia groves were suffering without fire. Fewer sequoias were able to grow. In the 1970s, the park began implementing controlled burns. These are fires that are intentionally started in specific areas. They are overseen so they don't get out of control. Today, park rangers regularly perform controlled burns. With the help of human management, Yosemite's ecosystems can continue to flourish as they have for thousands of years.

STRAIGHT TO THE SOURCE

Sandy Hernandez is Guatemalan American. She works with the National Park Service in Yosemite National Park. She said this about being a park worker of color:

> *The future of Yosemite doesn't just rely on biological diversity, but cultural diversity as well. And that's just as important. . . . We need more stewards of these lands to protect the outdoors, regardless of what your ethnic and racial background is. It's a team effort. . . . I didn't grow up seeing park rangers that look like me. But I'm here now and I try to make myself as visible as possible so that I can show others that they can fill this position, this role, and that they can dream as big as they can dream. . . . And once they get here, to sit at the table.*

Source: "Sandy Hernandez: No Us and Them in Nature." *National Park Service*, 23 Jan. 2023, nps.gov. Accessed 1 Oct. 2024.

BACK IT UP

The author of this passage is using evidence to support a point. Write a paragraph describing the point the author is making. Then write two or three pieces of evidence the author uses to make the point.

PARK LANDMARKS

Yosemite Falls is one of the tallest waterfalls in the United States. Visitors can hike to the waterfall's base and top.

El Capitan is a granite rock formation located in Yosemite Valley. Advanced rock climbers can climb up the sheer cliff face.

Bridalveil Fall is a 620-foot (190 m) waterfall in Yosemite Valley. Visitors can hike to the base of the waterfall.

Half Dome is a massive granite rock formation in Yosemite Valley. Three of its sides are rounded, with the fourth side being a steep vertical cliff.

Wawona Tunnel cuts through a granite mountain, taking visitors to Yosemite Valley. At the end of the tunnel is a famous overlook into the valley.

Mariposa Grove is located in the southern portion of Yosemite. It contains more than 500 sequoia trees, making it the largest sequoia grove in the park.

STOP AND THINK

Surprise Me

Chapter Two describes the early history of Yosemite National Park. After reading this book, what two or three facts about the park's early history surprised you? Write a few sentences about each fact. Why did you find each fact surprising?

Dig Deeper

After reading this book, what questions do you still have about Yosemite? With an adult's help, find a few reliable sources that can help you answer your questions. Write a paragraph about what you learned.

Take a Stand

Many American Indians lost their land in order for Yosemite to become a national park. Now, descendants of those American Indians are starting to become more involved in the park's management. Do you think native nations should have a say in how the park is managed today? Why or why not?

Say What?

Studying national parks can mean learning a lot of new vocabulary. Find five words in this book you've never heard before. Use a dictionary to find out what they mean. Then write the meanings in your own words and use each word in a new sentence.

GLOSSARY

alpine
relating to mountains

altitude
height above sea level

backcountry
wilderness

crystalline
resembling a crystal

diversity
variety

ecosystem
a community of organisms living together and interacting

extinction
the process of a species dying out completely

habitat
the natural home of a plant or animal

headwater
the starting point of a river

organism
a living thing

steward
a person who takes care of a specific place

vegetation
plants found in a particular habitat

ONLINE RESOURCES

To learn more about Yosemite National Park, visit our free resource websites below.

Visit **abdocorelibrary.com** or scan this QR code for free Common Core resources for teachers and students, including vetted activities, multimedia, and booklinks, for deeper subject comprehension.

Visit **abdobooklinks.com** or scan this QR code for free additional online weblinks for further learning. These links are routinely monitored and updated to provide the most current information available.

LEARN MORE

Alexander, Heather. *Only in California*. Wide Eyed, 2022.

Petersen, Christine. *Yosemite*. Fox Chapel, 2024.

Ward, Alexa. *America's National Parks*. Lonely Planet, 2024.

INDEX

About the Author

Emma Kaiser is a writer and educator based in western Minnesota. She has a Master of Fine Arts in creative writing from the University of Minnesota, and her writing has appeared in a number of magazines and publications. She is the author of several other nonfiction books for students.